D'Nealian® Handwriting from A to Z

Manuscript Capitals Practice

Donald N. Thurber

GOOD YEAR BOOKS

Pearson Learning Group

Contents

Good Year Books are available for most basic curriculum subjects plus many enrichment areas. For more Good Year Books, contact your local bookseller or educational dealer.

Book design and art by Nancy Rudd.

Developed in conjunction with Donald N. Thurber, creator of *D'Nealian ® Handwriting*, and Scott, Foresman and Company. D'Nealian is a registered trademark of Donald Neal Thurber.

ISBN 0-673-58908-0
Printed in the United States of America

3 4 5 6 7   08 07 06 05 04

1-800-321-3106
www.pearsonlearning.com

How to Teach the Letters

Why Teach Capital Letters?

Kindergarten teachers tell us that if children come to school able to print, they usually print exclusively in capital letters. Parents, grandparents, and caregivers, dealing with children who are strongly motivated to write "like big people," teach the print letters they use. Most adults use capital letters when asked to print.

The procedure usually followed in the classroom is to teach the lowercase manuscript letters first because children use more lowercase than capital letters in their writing. We suggest that you start with the first book in this series (*D'Nealian® Handwriting from a to z: Lowercase Manuscript Practice*) and then proceed with this book. Teachers expect children to learn how and when to use capital letters correctly so you might as well start them off in the right direction.

For Your Review

Capital letters are used at the beginning of sentences, for proper nouns such as names, places, organizations, and titles.

Examples:

At the beginning of sentences: He went to the movies often. **G**oing to the movies is his hobby.

Proper names: Peter Jensen; Barbara **L**ong; **S**kippy

Places: St. Louis, **M**issouri; **N**ew **Y**ork, **N**ew **Y**ork; **A**ustin, **T**exas

Organizations: The **A**merican **R**ed **C**ross; **T**he **P**arent **T**eacher **A**ssociation; **B**etter **B**usiness **B**ureau

Titles: The **S**ecret **G**arden; **D**r. **W**endy **W. M**organ; **A**unt **J**ane

Beginning writers' needs for knowing when to use capital letters will probably be continued to names and places. Don't overwhelm them at this time in the learning process.

To further help the learner, the capital manuscript letters are introduced in common stroke groups—first C, G O, Q, S; then I, L, T, J, U, H, K; next A, B, D, M, N, P, R; last E, F, Z, V, W, X, Y. (If you need to introduce any letters out of this order, just be sure to follow the stroke directions presented on page 58.) It is important for teachers—or anyone who is instructing and overseeing letter practice—to be sure that the letters are produced according to the stroke directions.

How to Teach Capital Letters

The procedure we suggest for teaching or presenting the capital letters is a skill-progressive one. First, tell your child the name of the child pictured on the first page of each two-page lesson. Spell the name, being sure to emphasize the words "Capital C, lowercase *a, r, l, o, s.*" Have your child repeat after you, pointing to each letter.

Then have the child trace with a finger the large letter near the picture. He or she can then progress to using a pencil for tracing the letters with arrows and starting dots. The next step in the process is to trace and write the letters without arrows or starting dots. Notice the size of the letters as the child works through the page. The letters are getting smaller. By the time the child writes the capital letters without arrows and starting dots, he or she will be writing at a rather adult-looking size.

At this point we suggest you use a separate sheet of paper and ask the child to review the lowercase letter for that capital letter. You should compare the capital and lowercase for size and form. Talk about the letters. *Which is bigger? Is the capital just a larger lowercase letter or is it different?*

As you begin page two of the letter lesson, ask the child to identify the first picture. It is the same child as the one on the previous page. Repeat the name and point to each letter as you spell it. Remember to use the terms *Capital* and *lowercase* as you spell the name. Ask the child to trace the first name on the lines with a finger and then with a pencil. Next, ask him or her to write the sample name under the model, paying particular attention to size and spacing. If the child produces a letter that looks all right, but you've noticed that he or she has not made it according to the stroke directions, stop and correct the formation immediately. The child will have fewer problems with letter mix-up if you follow this procedure.

At the bottom of the page are challenge words your child might try to form. Follow the procedure of pointing to the letters as you spell each name. Demonstrate any new formation, using the stroke directions from page 58. If the child becomes tired of writing, you might work on a list of names of friends and relatives to write at a later time—when the child is rested and better motivated.

Motivation and practice are key to success. Children are naturally motivated, and if you make the practice an enjoyable activity, success for all is assured.

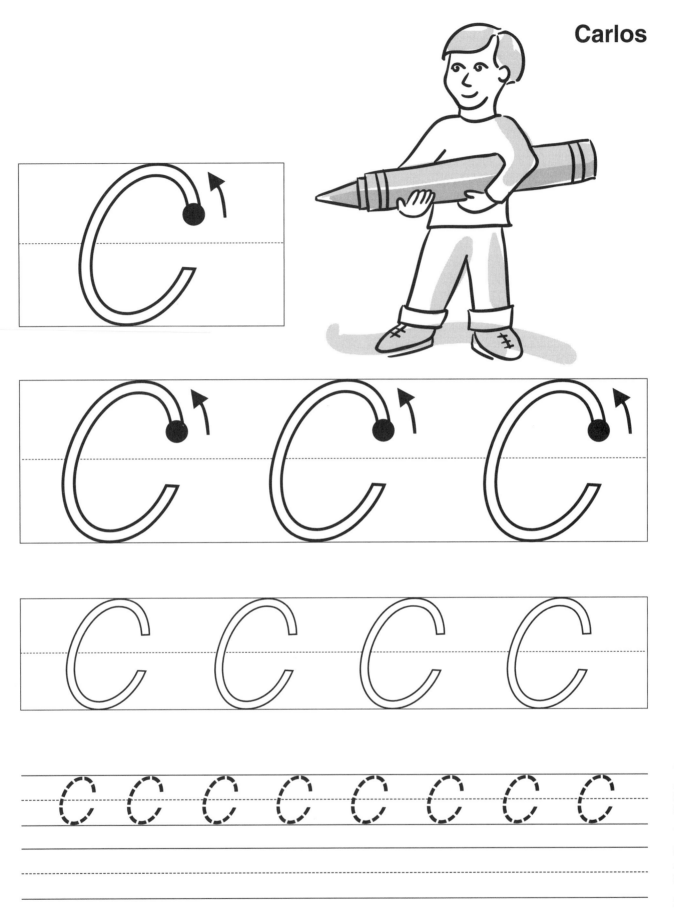

Carlos

Cary

Challenge Words

Chris

Connie

Cindy

Chicago

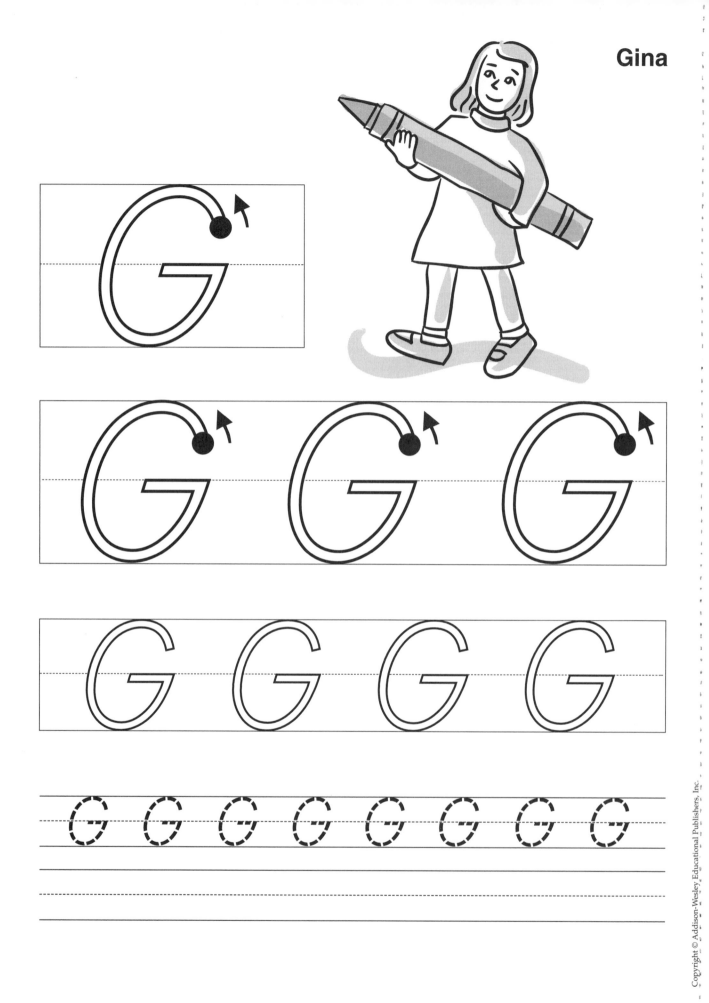

Gina

Gina

Greg

Challenge Words

Grandma

Grandpa

Gary

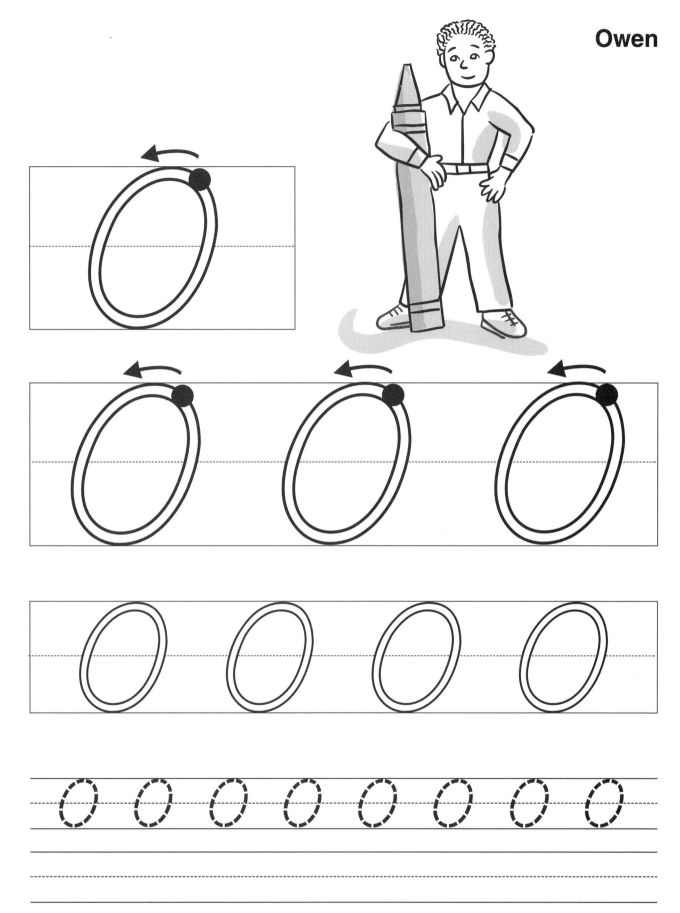

Owen

Ona

Challenge Words

Ohio

Ocean City

Olivia

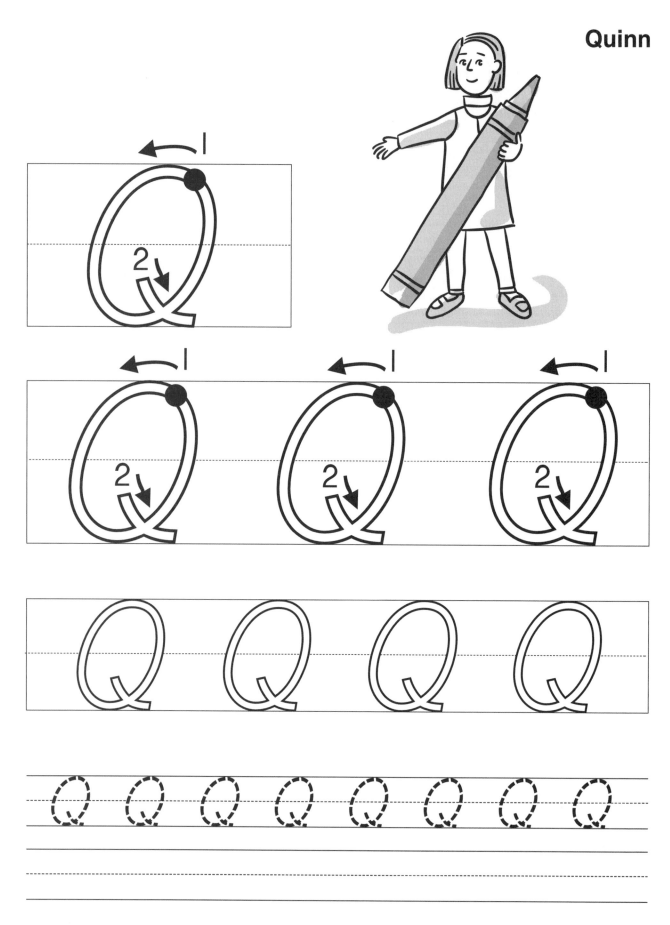

Quinn

Quentin

Challenge Words

Quincy

Queenie

Sara

S

S S S

S S S S

S S S S S S S S

D'Nealian® Handwriting from A to Z: Manuscript Capitals Practice

Sara

Steven

Challenge Words

Sunny

Socks

Seattle

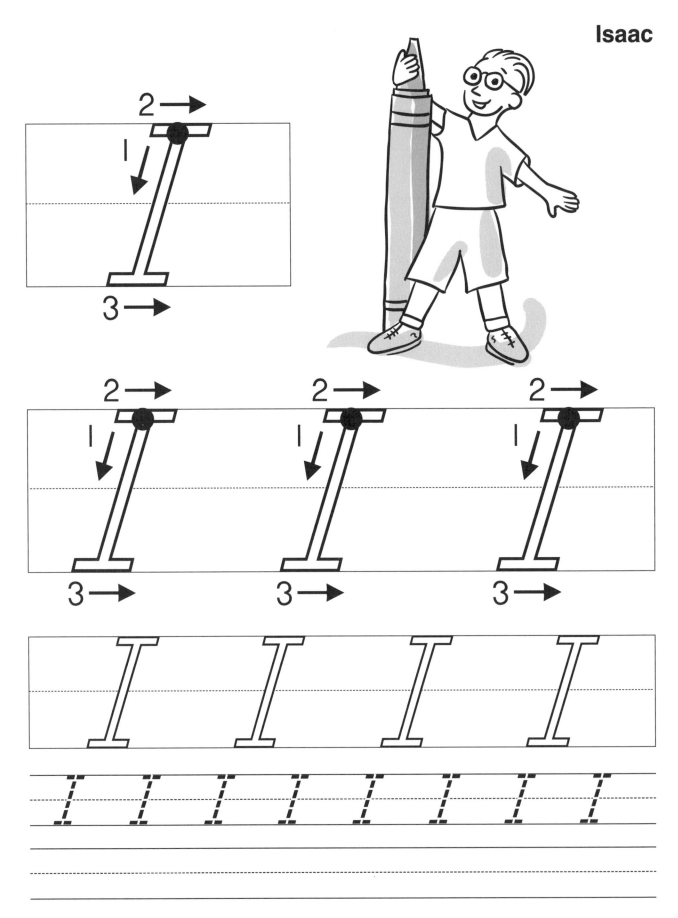

D'Nealian® Handwriting from A to Z: Manuscript Capitals Practice

Isaac

Inez

Challenge Words

Iowa

Idaho

Irene

D'Nealian® Handwriting from A to Z: Manuscript Capitals Practice

Latoya

Lee

Challenge Words

Lake Louise

Link

Leo

Lisa

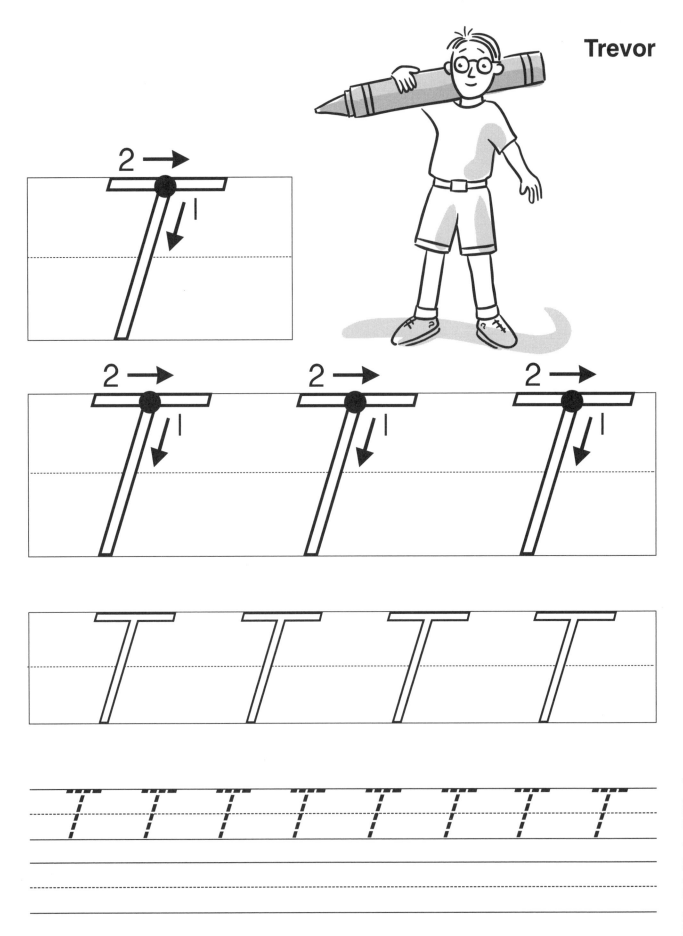

Trevor

D'Nealian® Handwriting from A to Z: Manuscript Capitals Practice

Trevor

Taylor

Challenge Words

Tina

Trenton

Troy

Jane

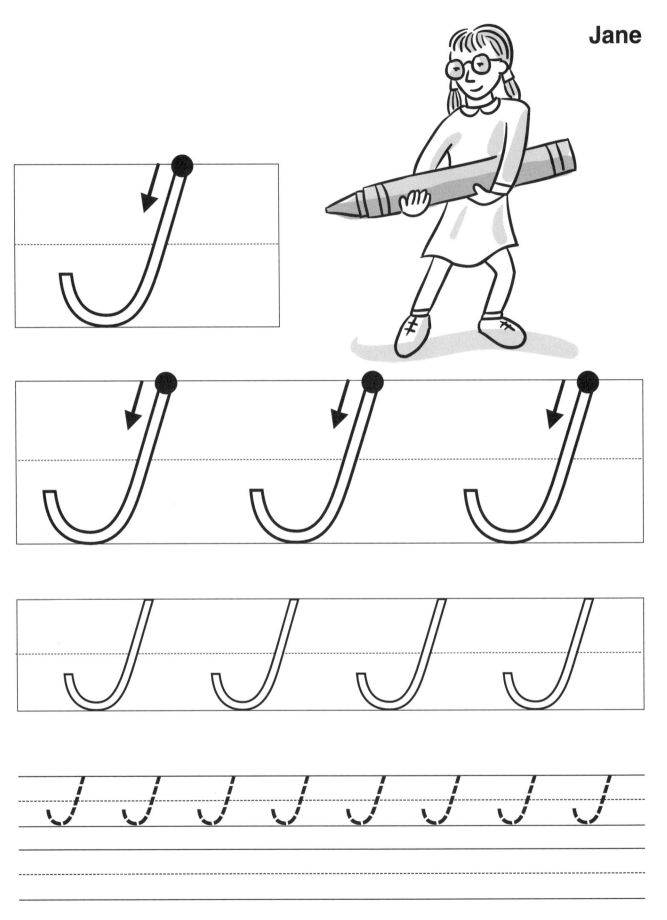

D'Nealian® Handwriting from A to Z: Manuscript Capitals Practice

Jane

James

Challenge Words

Jake

Jasper

Japan

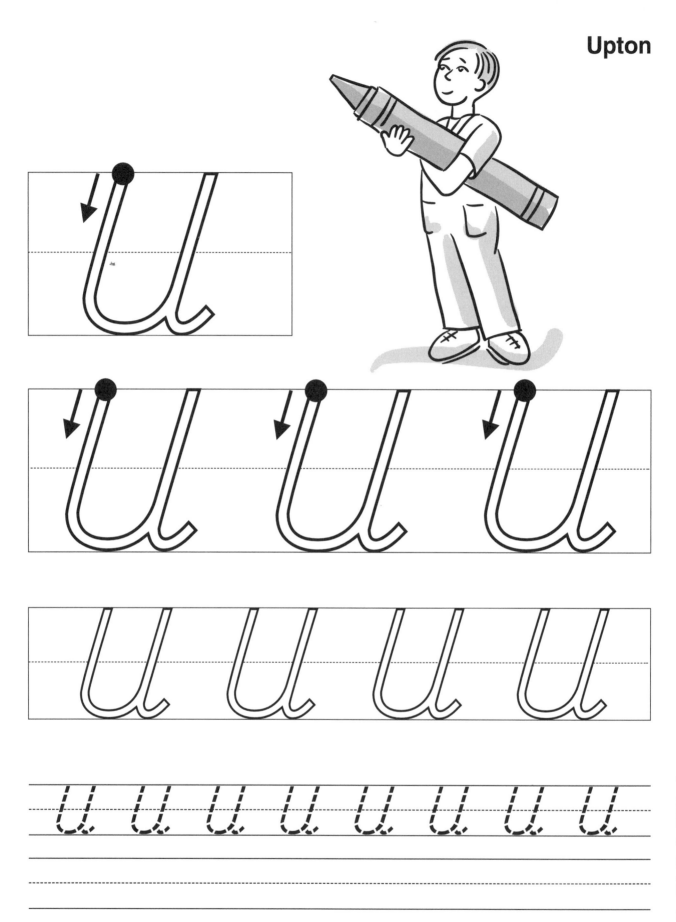

D'Nealian® Handwriting from A to Z: Manuscript Capitals Practice

Upton

Ursula

Challenge Words

Utah

Uncle Joe

Udell

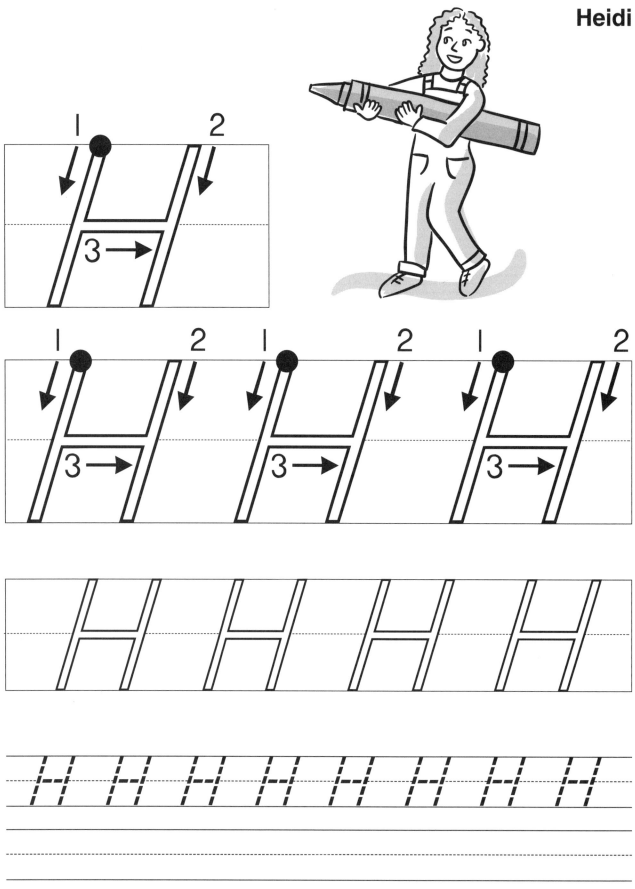

Heidi

Hector

Challenge Words

Hugo

Howie

Hannah

Kim

Kirk

Kirk

Challenge Words

Kerry

Kyle

Katie

D'Nealian® Handwriting from A to Z: Manuscript Capitals Practice **27**

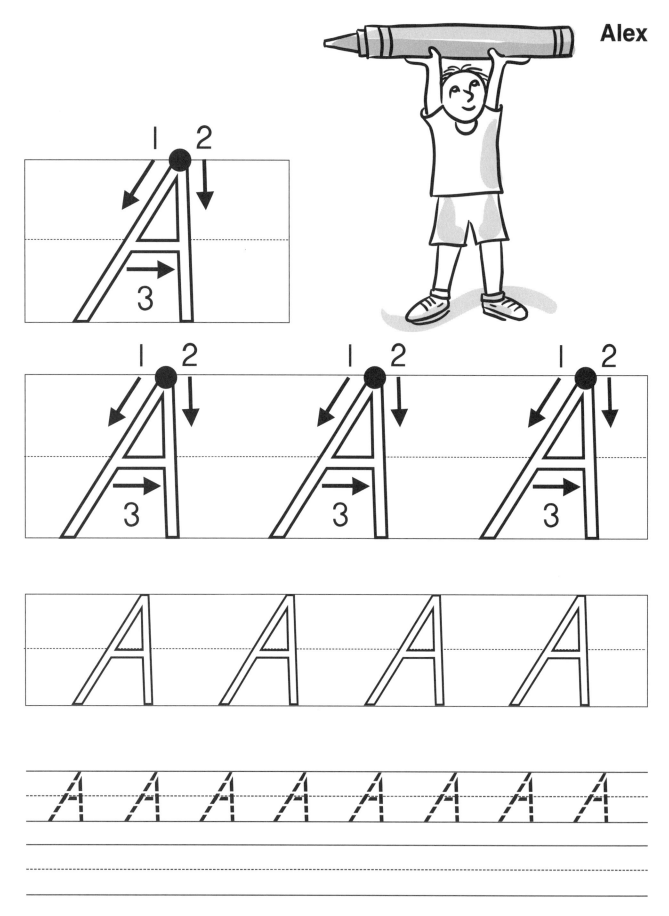

Alex

D'Nealian® Handwriting from A to Z: Manuscript Capitals Practice

Alex

Amy

Challenge Words

Amos

Aunt Ann

Adam

Beth

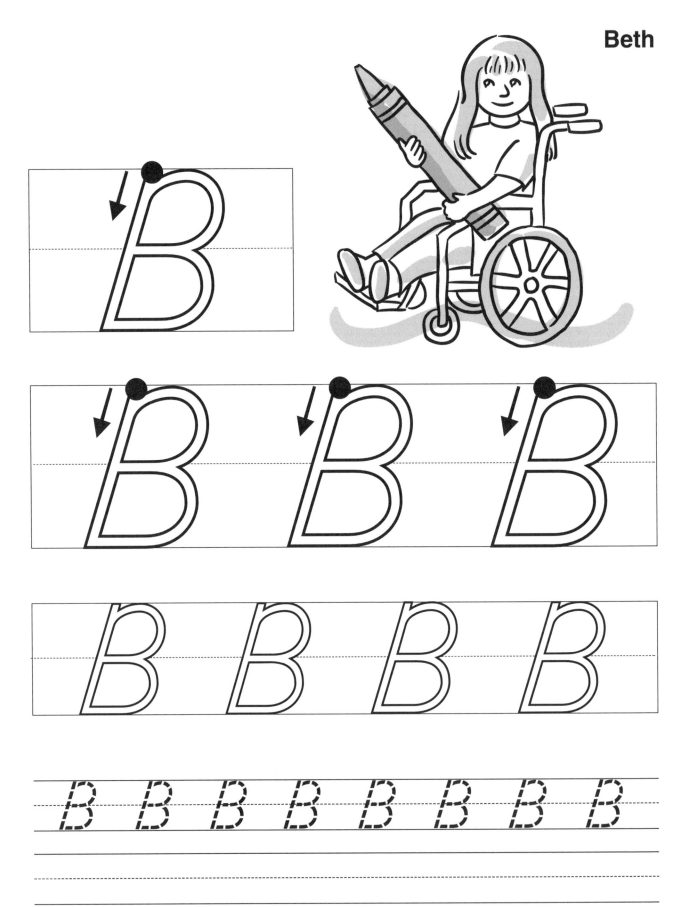

D'Nealian® Handwriting from A to Z: Manuscript Capitals Practice

Beth

Barry

Challenge Words

Barb

Boston

Bart

D'Nealian® Handwriting from A to Z: Manuscript Capitals Practice

David

Demita

Challenge Words

Dad

Daddy

Dustin

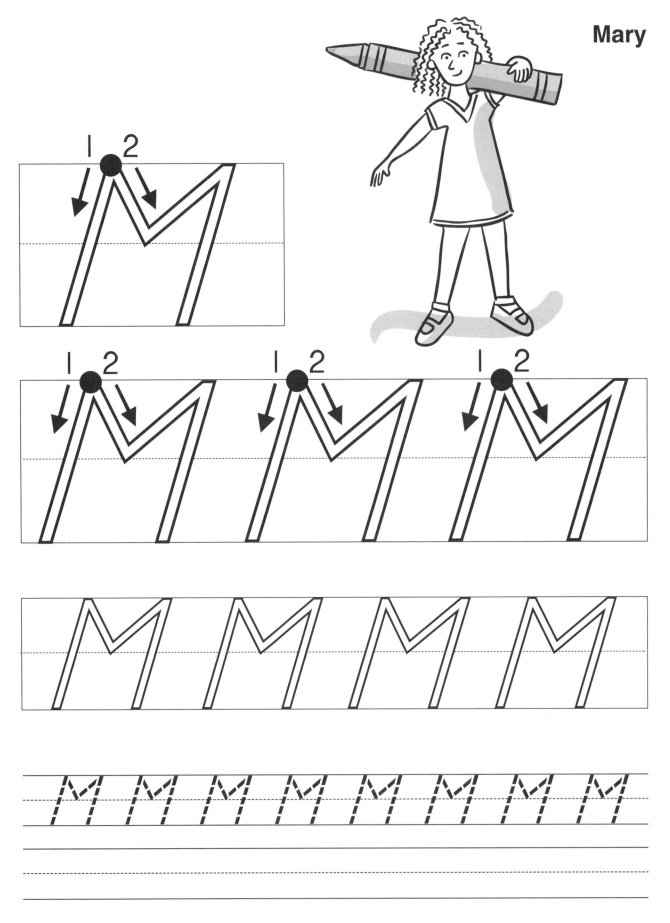

Mary

D'Nealian® Handwriting from A to Z: Manuscript Capitals Practice

Mary

Matthew

Challenge Words

Mom

Mommy

Mike

Ned

Nancy

Challenge Words

Nome

Newton

Neil

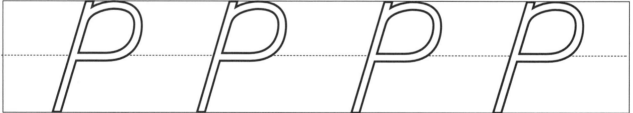

Pat

Pedro

Challenge Words

Paris

Paul

Penny

R

R R R

R R R R

R R R R R R R R R

Robert

Rachel

Challenge Words

Rock River

Rosa

Robin

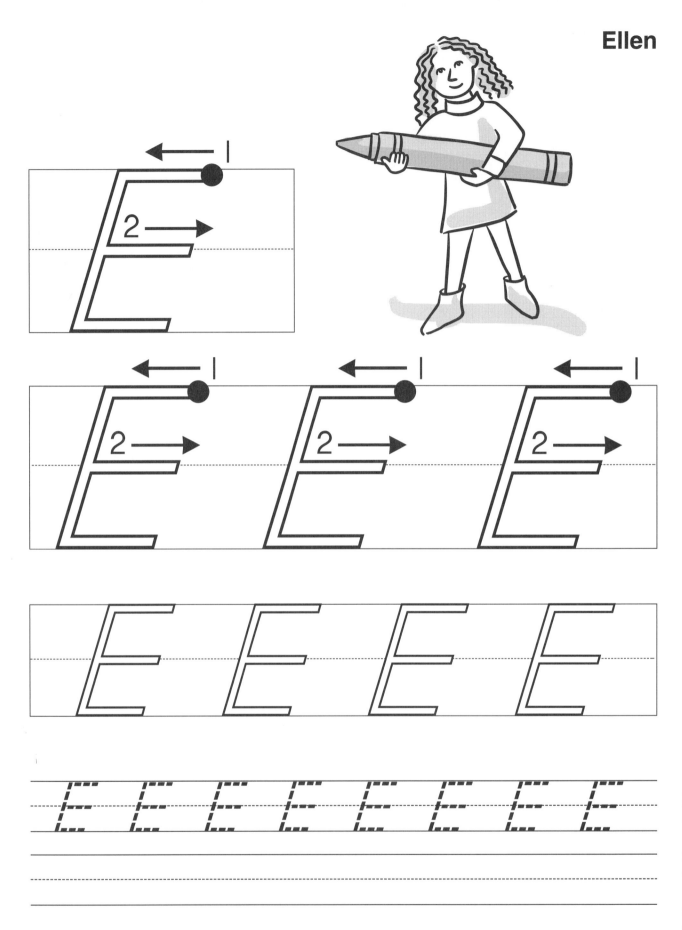

Ellen

Edward

Edward

Challenge Words

Edwin

Elm St.

Emily

Fredo

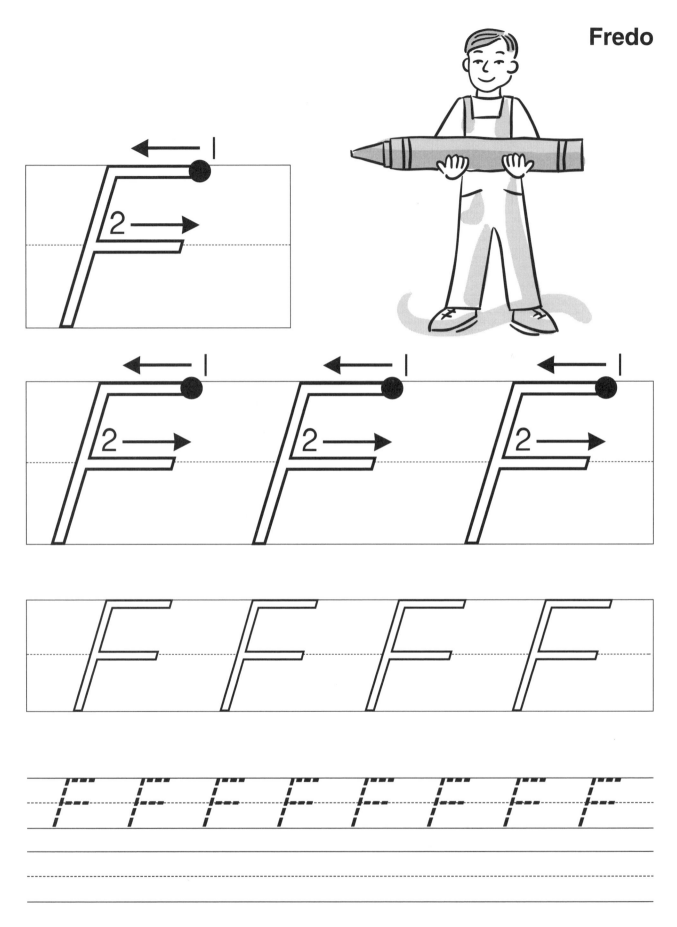

D'Nealian® Handwriting from A to Z: Manuscript Capitals Practice

Fredo

Felicia

Challenge Words

Fiona

Felix

Fresno

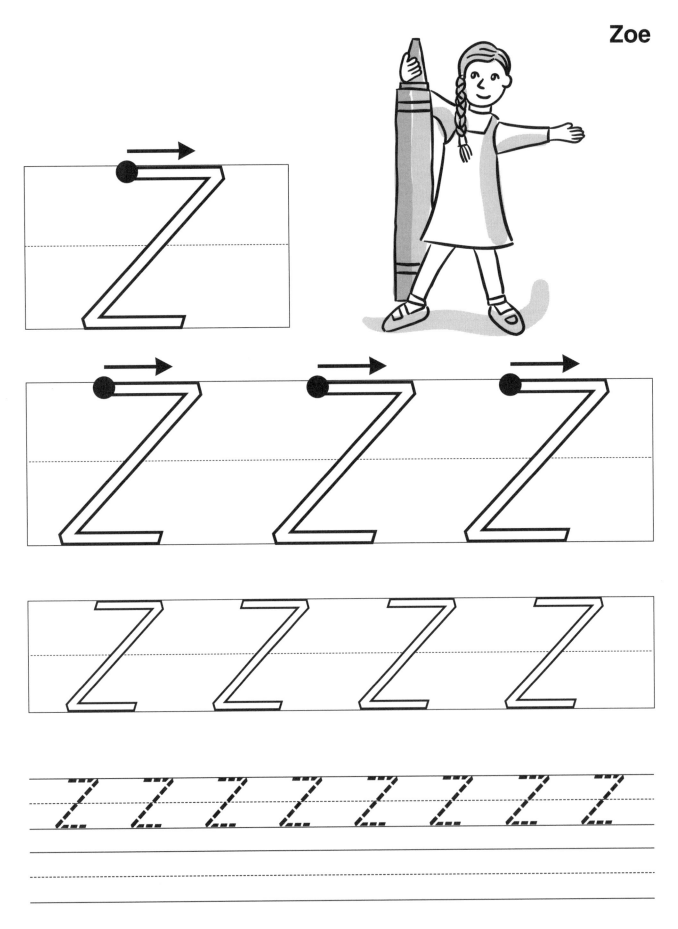

Zoe

D'Nealian® Handwriting from A to Z: Manuscript Capitals Practice

Zoe

Zack

Challenge Words

Zip Code

Zippy

Zara

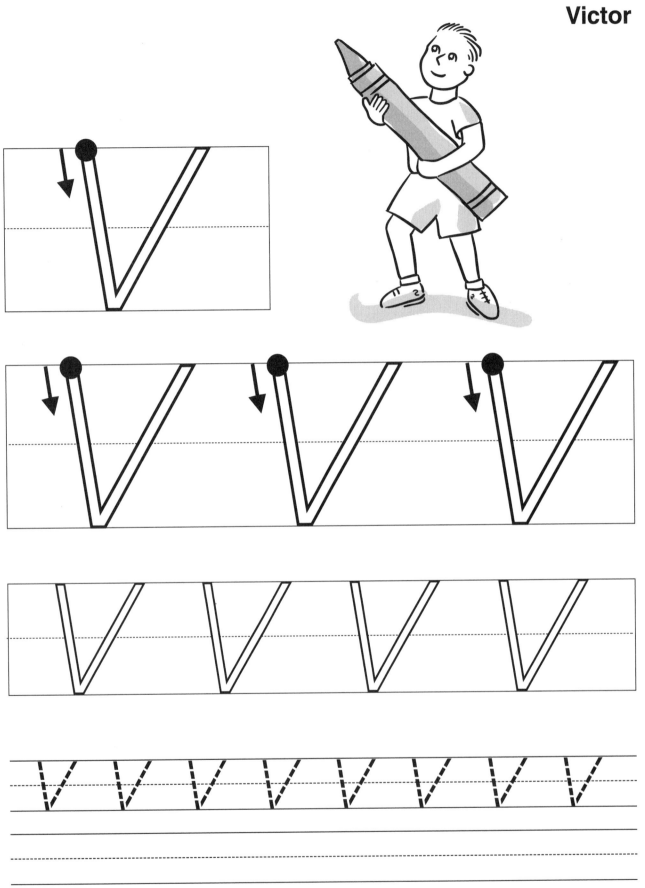

Victor

Valerie

Challenge Words

Valley St.

Vail Ave.

Vivian

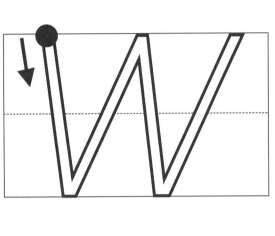

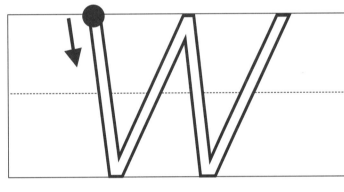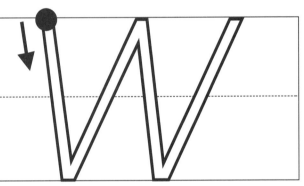

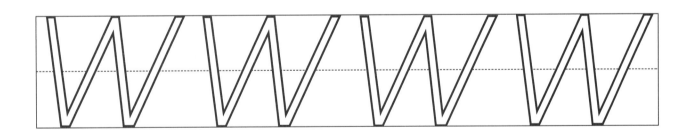

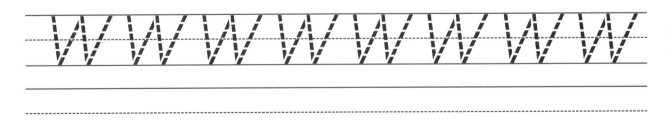

Wendy

William

Challenge Words

Wall St.

Will

Wayne

Xavier

D'Nealian® Handwriting from A to Z: Manuscript Capitals Practice

Xavier

Xiomara

Challenge Words

X-ray

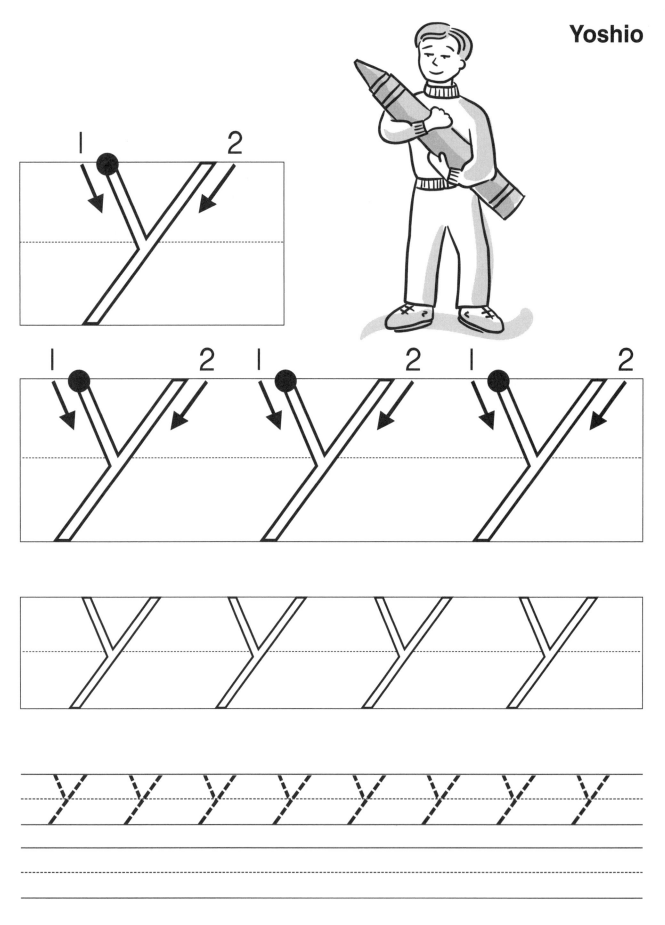

Yoshio

Yolanda

Challenge Words

Yellowstone

Yankees

York

Directions for Forming the Letters

A   Top start; slant down left. Same start; slant down right. Middle bar across.

B   Top start; slant down, up, around halfway, close, around again, and close.

C   Start below the top; curve up, around, down, up, and stop.

D   Top start; slant down, up, around, and close.

E   Top start; over left, slant down, and over right. Middle bar across.

F   Top start; over left, and slant down. Middle bar across.

G   Start below the top; curve up, around, down, up, and over left.

H   Top start; slant down. Another top start, to the right; slant down. Middle bar across.

I   Top start; slant down. Cross the top and bottom.

J   Top start; slant down, and curve up left.

K   Top start; slant down. Another top start, to the right; slant down left, touch, slant down right, and a monkey tail.

L   Top start; slant down, and over right.

M   Top start; slant down. Same start; slant down right halfway, slant up right, and slant down.

N   Top start; slant down. Same start; slant down right, and slant up.

O   Top start; around down, and close up.

P   Top start; slant down, up, around halfway, and close.

Q   Top start; around down, and close up. Cross with a curve down right.

R   Top start; slant down, up, around halfway, close, slant down right, and a monkey tail.

S   Start below the top; curve up, around, down and a snake tail.

T   Top start; slant down. Cross the top.

U   Top start; down, around, up, down, and a monkey tail.

V   Top start; slant down right, and slant up right.

W   Top start; slant down right, slant up right, slant down right, and slant up right again.

X   Top start; slant down right, and a monkey tail. Cross down left.

Y   Top start; slant down right halfway. Another top start, to the right; slant down left, and touch on the way.

Z   Top start; over right, slant down left, and over right.

A A A A A A A A A

B B B B B B B B

C C C C C C C C

D D D D D D D D

E E E E E E E E

F F F F F F F F

G G G G G G G G

H H H H H H H H

I I I I I I I I

J J J J J J J J

K K K K K K K K

L L L L L L L L

M M M M M M M M

D'Nealian® Handwriting from A to Z: Manuscript Capitals Practice

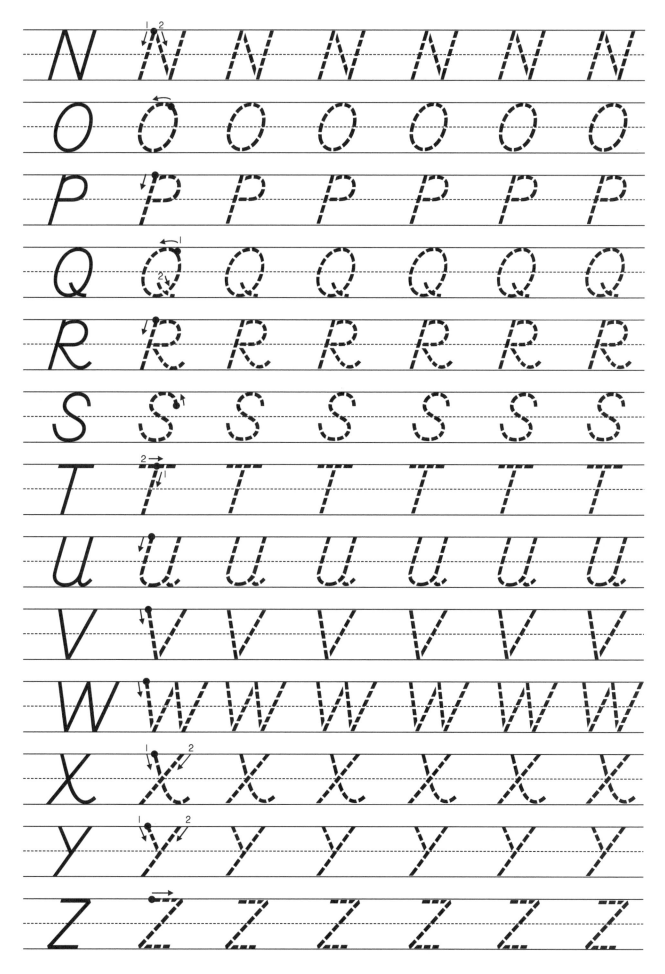

1

2

D'Nealian® Handwriting from A to Z: Manuscript Capitals Practice

3

4

5

6

D'Nealian® Handwriting from A to Z: Manuscript Capitals Practice

9

10

D'Nealian® Handwriting from A to Z: Manuscript Capitals Practice